CW00494329

PETER

A TOILET TRAINING BOOK

PAPA G

Hi, I'm Papa G and I am a normal parent.

You see that family over there that just road to the park on their pushbikes, dad at the front, mum bringing up the rear and two perfectly presented children in the middle. All packing nutritious bean and fruit lunches. No, that's not me. That's me over there, the guy with the kid snot on his shoulder. Pushing a swing with one hand and trying to open a juice box with the other. The guy who hasn't slept properly in years. Not one of those super-parents, just a normal parent... a Norm.

As a Norm, my wife and I fight daily battles. Battles of teeth brushing and putting on clothes, battles of eating, drinking and wiping butts, battles of trying to stop siblings killing each other and we are both veterans of two long campaigns of potty training.

The latest campaign was waged against my son; it was a campaign of dirty tricks and propaganda, a long campaign that had resulted in a bitter standoff. That is when Peter Poo came to the fray, like a mighty knight in shiny brown armour. A figment of my fevered, sleep deprived mind. I quickly grabbed some A4 from the printer and scribbled down the story, illustrating it myself. I then stapled it together and gave him the book as a present. He loved it!

Did it work? I hear you cry. Did it miraculously get my son to use the dunny? No, of course it didn't. We Norms know nothing is that easy when it comes to our kids. But what Peter Poo did do was to bring some humour and light relief to a tense situation. Initially my son would happily slam dunk his nappy into the bin with a "Bye Peter Poo" and every Thursday morning he would wave to the rubbish truck as it took poor Peter Poo to the tip. But the seed had been planted. Then one day he walked past without a word and went into the toilet. My wife and I held our breaths. A few minutes later he walked out with the toilet announcement. It was high fives all round. We could have cried we were so happy. Then we finally sent Peter Poo to swim with the fish.

Now you may read this book and say to yourself "I am just not that comfortable using emotional blackmail to get my little darling to use the toilet. It's just not right."

Well I say to you. Perhaps, just maybe, you are not a Norm.

Papa G (Proud Norm)

MY NAME IS PETER POO!

HOW DO YOU DO?

You Look Very Happy, Peter Poo!

THAT'S BECAUSE TODAY I GET TO DO WHAT I ALWAYS WANTED!

What's That Peter Poo?

I GET TO SWIM
WITH THE FISH IN THE SEA!

WHOO-HOO!

That Sounds Like FUN!

IT'S GOING TO BE

AWESOME!

How Will You Get There?

FIRST, I'M GOING TO JUMP
INTO THE TOILET.

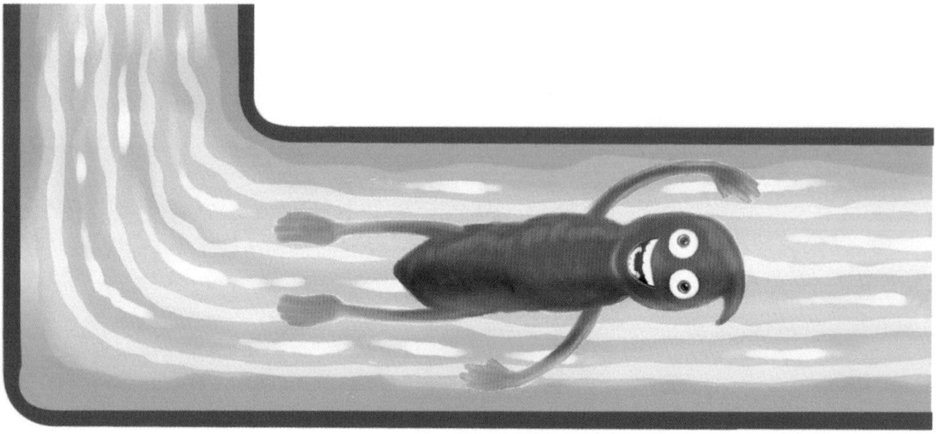

THEN I AM GOING TO SWIM DOWN
THE PIPE TO THE SEA.

Good Luck Peter Poo.
Have a Nice Trip!

Wait Peter Poo! Come Back,
It's a NAPPY!

I CAN'T STOP ONCE I'VE STARTED!

OH NO!

Poor Peter Poo! He's in a **NAPPY**!

Try To Hang On Peter Poo!

Stay Away From The Light!

Oh No! Where's He Going?

It's The Bin!

Oh No Now Where Are They Taking Him?!

The RUBBISH Truck!

IT'S DARK IN HERE!

Try To Hang On,
Peter Poo!

Oh! No Now They've Buried
Him In a Deep Dark Hole!

There's No Way That's Nicer Than Swimming With The Fish.

NO IT IS NOT.

HOW SAD.

Thank Goodness It Was Just a Dream! What a Relief!

IT WAS A **NIGHTMARE!**

But Why Do You Look So Worried, Peter Poo?

WHAT IF IT **IS** A NAPPY?

I DON'T WANT TO BE BURIED IN A STINKY HOLE!

PLEASE LET ME SWIM WITH THE FISH!

The END!

Printed in Great Britain
by Amazon

46053883R00016